139 Pages of Pining

aka

The (Better) Book of Longing

By Brody McVittie

aka Tragedy in Training

aka Exhausting since 1980

aka The first Rockstar writer since Chaucer

aka The Patron Saint of Sometimes

Table of Contents

Book 1: For the girl who's leaving.

Waiting for me to step up and be a man…..9

Does this even make sense?....10

The only Two Words that can stop me…….12

I suck!!!....13

Come visit me!....15

This One goes out to Girlfriend #17…..17

*Still less than the rest of me…..19

So you shift your weight, and it weighs on me…..20

Counting Curls….22

The Patron Saint of Sometimes….24

She's the type who tells you she doesn't like sad songs, right before she tells you it's over…..26

'Leaving' is a four-letter word…..29

Things she says to me (in and around the things she says to me)….30

The Latest Thing I Dislike About You….33

The Latest in a List of things I'll never say to You….34

I don't even know what the fuck an Ottoman is….36

'Failure' starts with my favorite letter….38

Today's break-up is brought to you by the letter 'G'….39

Exhausting Since 1980….41

The Alchemy of Me….45

Before You leave (for the thousandth fucking time)….46

4

5,368,232 words, for two....48

> *Book 2: For the girl who's gone.*

"..."....50

Of Going The Way You Go.....51

Another over-elaborate way of saying something....52

Normal, and other things I used to be....54

Thank your lucky stars I'm not published.....57

Of all the things I'm addicted to, you taste best....59

Baby, everybody has a talent or two....60

Tuesday, for your information, is still cheap night.....61

(More) Fun With Numbers.....62

Ten digits deep.....63

B is for Burden....65

Me, and other things you left (when you left).....67

'Unfixable' is just a buzz-word for Broken.....68

June 19, 2006, and here you are.....69

Really, 'fire' is the only element we didn't lack....71

Sick, yeah, but with an 'l' in it (--so 'slick.').....72

Here's to War, and waging it.....75

Words we used To, For, Against & About one another...76

More of the things Time (and his friend Tequila) makes me miss.....77

Intent vs. The Shit That Comes Out Of Your Mouth.....79

The Sin of Something Else.....82

'Promise' is a four-letter word....84

Creative Uses of My Favorite Word....85

(Two things that don't necessarily go well together.)....86

Time, and other tiny tragedies....87

Sightings and shit....89

Damn, if I don't sense a pattern....90

I win.....92

Similes, I guess....93

Twisting tongues and feelings.....94

Second Place is for losers and Indianapolis Colts.....96

Take your jar of insecurities, and—....98

Names, and other things I called you....99

Day Four....102

Something clever I came up with, waiting to not wait for you (anymore.)....105

Something you said, I guess, reminded me of something Pa used to say....107

Grain.....109

Today I spell sadness _ _ _ _ _
(A.I.M.E.E).....113

Gorillas and Ghosts.....119

... Don't Worry Ma; It's A Metaphor....120

No further down....121

Things I Miss Most
(As Told By the Ten-Year-Old You Turned Me Into)....124

Speaking of Analogies....125

Book 3: For the girl who's stupid enough to stay.

Close that fucking door — there's a draft coming in.....127

You might be taking this the wrong way.....129

Of Scars and Ones who Scarred Me.....131

More buzzwords for broken.....132

And you say I never write about you.....134

Other couples say it's the cutest thing about us!....136

Truths Rolled In And Around Ego.....137

What I've learned, after looking back at all of this....139

Book 1: For the girl who's leaving.

...

Waiting for me to step up and be a man.

She turns to me, and she says

I can't live this way anymore.

So I look at her, and I say

Hold your breath, baby, and I'll get us out

And then I look away

and I hope to God

She's got the lung capacity.

...

...

Does this even make sense?

She says I'll never be good enough

in breaths and between

the breaths she breathes

away from me.

And she says she just

knows,

you know,

the way you know

when you look in the eyes of the one

you waited for;

waited for, for maybe just a little too long.

So I take the hit on the chin

like it came from Tyson

then;

on my way down

to the ground

she's grounding me on,

I'm thinking of ways

I'll pick myself back up.

But up is down

and I'm on the ground,

just the latest in a line

of lines she feeds me

in between the breaths she breathes

away from me.

...

12

The only Two Words that can stop me...

Let

and

Go.

...

I suck!!!

And you're the latest

in a line of things I've failed to conquer;

So congrats on being elusive,

like the high score in Donkey Kong

or

passing that Grade 10 math

or

anything, really, that has to do with loving

or

not-loving

the rest of you attached to that smile

and

those eyes

and

that ass.

And all I can really do

is reflect

and

wonder

what book I have to bury my head in

to finally be able to

make the grade

and

be the boy

that succeeds in really, really

really

breaking you down, too.

Come visit me!

I live

foot planted firmly in the past

At the cost of my present,

I know

And probably my future, too

if I fail at this

the way I am

The way I remain completely utterly unremarkable

on the off chance

that yourself or someone like you

reads this

And saves my life

the way I've been drowning and

trying to save yours.

...

This One goes out to Girlfriend #17.

I remember

the split-second I broke your heart;

some seconds south

of the time you looked at me

for the second time

with that

'I-told-you-so'

look;

telling me

without telling me

that breaking is all I'm really good at

and letting me down easy

some seconds south

of letting you down, too.

...

*Still less than the rest of me.

Okay, I should have gone after you

but chasing

is the opposite of running away;

and either

way

my feet hurt. *

...

So you shift your weight, and it weighs on me.

So you shift your weight

the way you do when you're sad

and it weighs on me

after you go the way you

go

when it hurts too bad.

Hurts, like that time in tenth grade

a girl named Summer left my heart

broken and bruised among Autumn leaves

she taught me the meaning of lives lived apart.

And the sting is back

in the back of my throat and somewhere south

watching you go the way you

go

already missing the taste in your mouth.

It moves, your mouth

on your way out the door

you shift your weight and you look over your

shoulder

and you promise me

before you go

that it will ever and always sting more.

...

Counting Curls

She's got at least

two hundred and four

curls

that I count

while she sleeps

when she sleeps

beside me.

(--And no, you don't find that creepy.)

It's clever, more,

and it shows, kinda,

the kinda guy I was before;

the guy who could stay

awake and away

counting curls on her head

while she sleeps in my bed.

Now I'm watching

curls

walk out my door

and I'm sad again

just like

before;

I lose another

left to wonder

how many more?

...

The Patron Saint of Sometimes

So I guess I'm

The Patron Saint of Sometimes;

Sometimes I'm good enough

Sometimes I'm man enough

Sometimes, she swears,

*she might-*maybe *even love me.*

Sometimes I work

out in the Wild and the Wind,

and Sometimes she says

the Wild's in me

and that's why she's Gone With The;

like that old movie

and Sometimes I wish

25

I wasn't running out of stairways

to call her back down from.

...

She's the type who tells you she doesn't like sad songs, right before she tells you it's over.

She's the kind

who's really just not.

She'll give you the eyes that say

stay

before pushing her lips to say

go away.

And she'll turn her head

just a little to the left;

and the look, you think, is just right

and you wonder where to take her next

and she's waiting for you to take her home

so she can tell you goodnight.

So you move closer

because it's time and you've put in the

time

and she tells you it will take time

and much more

time

before the time you move your lips against her lips

when she moves her lips

and not against yours

moves her lips to tell you

over dinner you're paying for

that it will take dinners

and many many more.

She's every sad song

on the radio on the way home;

and the curves in the road

have you picturing hers

the way you will tonight

alone.

...

'Leaving' is a four-letter word.

And it's still dark

and there's no light

and I toss and turn

'cuz we fuss and fight

and not for the ways

I wish I could say

That would make you stay

just one more day.

...

30

Things she says to me (in and around the things

she says to me)

She says to me

in and around the things she says to me

that she grew up thinking men

were like the men

she grew up watching on TV.

Men like Kirk

comma Captain;

and men she grew up reading about

men like Captain

fucking America.

So she says to me

in and around the things she says to me

that I'm maybe half and less

the kind of man

she needs me to be.

And it hurts and more

than the fists that follow

the words that hit me

a half second and harder

than her fists and the look behind them;

the look that says

she's leaving,

leaving like the blood that runs

from the nose she breaks

not pumping her brakes

32

on her way out the door

to the next man

the next man

and his 'more.'

...

look me in my eyes

and tell me every last one of them

isn't

to

for

about

and

of

you.

...

36

I don't even know what the fuck an Ottoman is.

I'm on the ottoman

and Ambien

TM

and I'm thinking

--yeah, I really am —

about all the atrociously awful

extra crispy chicken shit

shit

you said to me

minutes before

you and your

minute little frame

bolted out my

door frame

taking pictures of us

framed or not

and putting them

where you put our love

somewhere lower than the shelves

we shelved our framed pictures

and inhibitions on

back when we decided

to share couches

with ridiculous names

...

'Failure' starts with my favorite letter.

She tells me I've failed

as a man.

I say,

Baby,

its okay,

the only tests I ever flunked

were the ones that mattered anyway.

...

Today's break-up is brought to you by the letter

'G'

So come on use your words

cuz baby we're not that old

and there's still plenty of time

and plenty of lies

in our story

yet to be told.

So come on use your words

any which ones you choose

pretty words like leave and again and away

words that all mean

lose.

Like I will

when you use your word for last

time

and then the time comes far too fast

to hold you and stop you the way I

should;

hold you

and

stop you

the way

any real man would.

...

Exhausting Since 1980

She tells me I'm exhausting,

I say

Bitch!

I say

I've been Exhausting Since 1980.

I tell her I've trademarked that,

she tells me I've trademarked being the most

unreasonable mess

she's ever, ever messed with.

She tells me to

Beat It!

So I say

Bitch!

I say

I'm gonna beat it like Rihanna

should,

(and I mean beat it from the boy who beat her.)

And can you blame me?

I mean, I'm on tap to be

the first Rockstar Writer since Chaucer

(and I trademarked that, too, I tell her)

and she tells me

I'll amount to less

than the half *a man*

she tells me I am

before she tells me to

Beat It!

again.

So I just

Beat It!

Beat It!

right out that

Bitch!

's

door,

'cuz even though I'm not a

(lower case)

rockstar

yet,

I'm on tap to be bigger

than those before.

...

The Alchemy of Me

She tells me I take things

And I take it hard

And she tells me hard is how I take

the things I tend to take;

things like dreams and ambitions and futures

And she tells me these are the things I would realize

if I stopped to take the time;

She tells me all of this

And I just sit there and take it.

...

Before You leave (for the thousandth fucking time)

You can leave

and I won't stop you;

You can say

the things you'll say

about the boy I am

about the man I'm not

Things you used to say

to yourself in whispers

you can say louder now

before you go away

Just please, one last thing

before you say the things

you stayed to say;

look me in the eyes

and then

try

to walk away.

...

48

5,368,232 words, for two.

don't. go.

Book 2: For the girl who's gone.

50

"..."

You always said

the pain made the writing better;

congratulations,

today I'm fucking Shakespeare.

...

Of Going The Way You Go.

Writing is getting harder

and

not

writing is getting easier

and

any which way you look at it

you're gone;

and

this dream I had

of making a career of it

is well on its way

chasing you out my door.

Another over-elaborate way of saying something

There was something you said

once

and

without saying anything at all, really;

something said that stayed

long after you did;

something said, and sadly

with your eyes and the wild in them

and without your lips and the words between them;

something that sounded

sweetly

and in passing,

something like

'I-believe-in-you'

when no one else would or could or, I guess

even should;

so I just want you to know

that every word I ever wrote

and every word I ever will

is really just my round-about way of saying

something like

'Thanks.

Normal, and other things I used to be

I used to have this sweater.

And I used to be normal, you know

Ten Fingers, Ten Toes.

I used to root for Jordan in the finals

and I used to tell myself,

'It's okay, tomorrow's another day'

I used to like ice cream

the way, I imagine, polar bears like snow days

I used to color outside the lines

and I used to want to

And then I met you

and then the things I used to want

I didn't want half as bad

as how bad — bad — I wanted you

So I used to have this sweater

And yeah, you know the one

You used to say it smelled like me

Hell, you used to want it to

Too, the way you wanted me

Not half as bad, apparently

as I wanted you

You took more than my sweater

But I suppose you figured that out

When you left me, down and

Left me to polar bears and snow days

And coloring outside of lines;

There's not many I wouldn't have crossed for you

If you'd given me time

And you can take that knowledge too

But please,

please

I'm begging you

--mail me back my fucking sweater.

...

Thank your lucky stars I'm not published.

'cuz you like to play it

close to the vest;

and you swear at me

when you see me

and you swear everywhere else

that you're over it;

telling me

'I'm over it'

but you lie

and it's in those eyes

swearing sweetly

You're only sometimes always on my mind

You're only sometimes always on my mind

You're only sometimes always on my mind.

...

Of all the things I'm addicted to, you taste best.

Better than the coke, and the booze

and

the pills and the girls

and the girls and the girls

I take and I drink and I take

to make myself

something other than

completely and utterly

fucked

without you.

...

Baby, everybody has a talent or two.

Well, excuse me

if

missing you

is the only thing

I've ever been

really, really

really

good at.

...

Tuesday, for your information, is still cheap night.

Memories are my favorite movies

'cuz our story got it right;

and if I still had the

right

to call or talk or text

I'd mention

maybe and in passing

that the days I pass through

don't mean half as much

muted and projected on some screen

sitting there and remembering

how we did it first, and better.

(More) Fun With Numbers

One thing you should know;

if I'm still three-quarters crazy

then that leaves a quarter talent —

--so the next time you're out

*with him or **him** or, heaven forbid,*

him —

remember that me at 75%

is better than 95% of him(s)

110% of the time.

...

Ten digits deep.

You should know

that every number I never dialed

on every night I should have known better

was yours and yours alone.

And you should know

that I can lift worlds across these shoulders

and hold them there

in the forever between phone calls.

But when it comes to finding the strength

to push the buttons that will bring you back

my hands shake and

my fingers fail.

And you should know

that it's no excuse and yet

it's my latest

And you should know

that when you rest the ear you listen with

on the pillow I'm not next to

that I'm still

so very sorry.

B is for Burden

And B

is what she

used to call me,

B-4

she walked out the door

B-cuz, she said, she couldn't stay any more.

And it's a little B-cuz

I'm so fucking poor

and a little B-cuz

there's holes

in my floor.

C

it'd be easy for me

to just call her a 'whore'

and pretend like

I don't love her no more,

but the truth is--

--the truth is —

--fuck it,

I'm out of words that rhyme.

Fuck her.

Me, and other things you left (when you left).

And all you couldn't stand

is all I ever wanted

And all you left behind

is all I'll ever have

So I guess you could say

'Linger' is my ALPHA-adjective

just another word

wasted on ears not yours

Alone (in company)

in the wake you left

when you went the way you went,

SO...

'Unfixable' is just a buzz-word for Broken.

And broken is how you left me

And broken is all I am

Like that toy in the toy chest

I loved just NORTH

of really, really loving you

He-Man is unfixable

And I'm unfixable, too

Unfixable

Unfixable

Unfixable

Ever chasing after

You.

June 19, 2006, and here you are.

I STILL, just so you know.

Still seven digits, odds and evens, if you're interested.

Still breathe a little faster, a step slower — for the record, heart still stops.*

(*Almost forgot, in the time since, just how much that hurts.)

Still wake up,

same side, same bed,

pictures bleeding out of my head

Technicolor red,

trailing the green of the same toothpaste

down the drain of the place you run from.

Pictures of days feeling less like memories, more like SOMETHING ELSE.

Still, though, six years removed.

Still relate the song on the radio to the smile on that Thursday,

a Thursday less a memory.

You remember, still, standing there, or are the feelings written on your face

for the tall, dark, and handsome guy over my shoulder?

You still, just so you know.

Still smell cinnamon sugar, hibiscus, and soul — ten manicured toes, and all that.

Still look like the first day,

the day after

and days since.

Still...

Really, 'fire' is the only element we didn't lack.

And the fuel we used

to light the fires

we'd fight

when we'd fight

fires, and

can't compare

to the fuel

I find

looking back at

pictures of you

in and amongst the ash and the wreckage

we called our relationship.

Sick, yeah, but with an 'l' in it (--so 'slick.')

Well baby,

if my words

have pain in and around them

then my voice

has ten kinds of cancer.

And you call yours

Mike,

because he never calls

when he says he'll call.

And you call yours

Ken,

because he left you

when you needed him

to go the other direction.

But when I call

my voice needs chemo

and my words

are sicker still;

spoken in tongues

better suited

for tickling yours.

Before, after and around

leaving my name

all over your

tongue,

having tasted ten

still yearning for the sick

my voice still carries

on the tip —

--pushing words and pain

through teeth

better suited

for fumbling with your

tongue and

teeth between.

Here's to War, and waging it.

And you lied when you said

that my wounds would mend

And you lied when you swore

you'd be back for me someday

You should know, I wasn't lying

when I said the wars I've waged

in your name and wake

number in the thousand thousands;

And you should know, I wasn't lying

when I swore to wage

a thousand thousand more.

Words we used To, For, Against & About one another

I used the word

stay

three-thousand, four-hundred twenty-two and a half

times,

in the three-thousand, four-hundred twenty-two and

a half

fights we fought;

apparently,

I should have used it

once

more.

More of the things Time (and his friend Tequila)

makes me miss.

I miss writing

and

Thundercats on Saturday mornings.

I miss something for nothing

and

that feeling I used to feel

when I felt I was doing something

maybe

worth doing.

I miss my hairline,

and

that quarter I lost under some couch somewhere.

Yeah, for the thousand-thousandth time,

I miss you;

but

I don't miss you

half as much

as I motherfucking

miss me.

Intent vs. The Shit That Comes Out Of Your Mouth.

You say

with your mouth and your hips and your finger and

all that ass

that I'm not

good enough and strong enough and smart enough

and

(goddamn it)

good looking enough.

You say

with your actions and your intent and your scent

and your

lack of

common sense

that I'm lacking in the qualities and the compassion

and the comprehension

and the...

well, the something else *you say I don't have,*

in and amongst the things you're saying;

and I'm looking into your eyes

and trying not to smile

and not *saying*

(--because, despite what you say, I'm smarter than that--)

that you can go on and

say

all the things I'm not.

Your eyes say something else,

something that makes me smile,

say,

Yeah,

I love you, too.

The Sin of Something Else.

If I've written a thousand thousand words

then I've written

a thousand thousand words

for you.

If I've broken a hundred hundred hearts

then I've broken

a hundred hundred hearts

because you broke mine.

And if I could trade a million million nights

to go back to that one

Then I'd look in your eyes

and save them all.

I'd tell you I love you

the way I've been trying to,

Every word and heart broken

in the million million nights

since the night

I said something else instead.

'Promise' is a four-letter word.

I promise

I've broken

more than my share.

I promise

I'm nowhere closer

to close enough.

I promise

you can write it on my tombstone

Because I promise

somewhere beneath it

or somewhere above it

I'm thinking of you.

Creative Uses of My Favorite Word

Fuck I look good

without a shirt.

And fuck if I haven't

fucked my fair share

But fuck if I'm not

just fucking fucked

For fucking it up

the way I fucked it up

with you.

(Two things that don't necessarily go well together.)

We don't get along

cats and vacuum cleaners

and the home we built

is a six-by-nine with bars

but the bar I found you in

is the bar I left you in

and the bars we skipped between

meant something more than the nothing

nights without you

left me to

when you left me, too.

Time, and other tiny tragedies.

I'm still me

and

You're still you;

It's just time

that's tried to take

the memories and moments

but time

is just one more thing

that couldn't come close

and

time

is just one more thing

that can fuck right off.

Sightings and shit

So I saw you the other day

You were walking the other way

So away

and walking

You caught me watching

the way you walk

when you walk the only way

you've walked since

you went away

the way you've walked

since I said

stay.

Damn, if I don't sense a pattern

And damn if I don't remember

that afternoon some September

You came into my memory

And my mind

catching eyes and

thoughts

and the thoughts that follow

the eyes that follow you

absorbing your scent

and intent

on your way across

from me

and into me

and my memory;

walking my way

and then away

taking September

everywhere but with you

and

leaving me to my memories

of how much I miss you.

I win.

Kiss me

Tell me

Fuck me

Maim me

Twist me

Make me

Leave me

Break me

Still can't

Shake me.

Similes, I guess

When it comes to this writing shit

I'm colder than you're step father.

Twisting tongues and feelings.

You manage to know

One hurt me so;

I dwell

as days go by

And you wonder why

I never reply

Just kind of sigh

Its like,

you say

I won't even try.

I hurt some too, you know

You remind me so

The lists in your mind

following words just unkind.

But lists are for groceries,

and some were just mean;

I dwell on a few

--leaving hurt girls--

to memories,

and cracks in between.

96

Second Place is for losers and Indianapolis Colts.

I used to call you

And

I used to call you 'sugartits' when I called you;

And

your new man calls you

And your new man calls you 'princess' when he calls

you

So that's the difference between us

(well, that and the penis)

So settle for second

and count them too;

until you see me across some bar

And

realize that, no, second just won't do.

Take your jar of insecurities, and —

Hold your insecurities

up to the light

I bet you've got enough

to fill a jar.

Go on, fill it up

be sure to twist that lid tight,

you wouldn't want any to escape.

Take your jar full of insecurities

and put it up on the shelf

between your bottle of dreams

and your flask

of tiny little infidelities.

Names, and other things I called you

I can't take back

The words I said or

The names I called you or

The feelings you felt

because

I called you;

but if you could

remember

the first time

I called you

The way you felt

then

is the way I feel

now and still;

And if you'd

call

I think you'd find

my words

on the other end

said

maybe just a little

more sweetly

in between

Sorry

might hide names like

baby

right before

and again around

the words I'll say

when I say

Come home.

Day Four

So they say

it takes fourteen days

to kick a habit.

Here's day four

(hundred and more)

and kicking

memories of you

is harder than

the habits I kicked

to hold you

and down

like we used to be.

I can honestly say

I'd rather kick coke

the highs were less

the lows much more

watching and waiting

behind closed doors.

Steroids, I could go without

knowing no matter the size

knowing no matter the swell

I'll always feel small

here in this hell.

Heroin, they say,

laughs at fourteen;

well, Heroin never spent the night

in your sheets and your eyes

kissing the magic I'll miss

in between your thighs.

I took a handful

of Vicodin;

washed it down

with Ambien

couldn't drown

while drowning

flashes of my front door

and the sunlight that followed

you through on days

before you were through with me

Something clever I came up with, waiting to not wait

for you (anymore.)

There are reasons

she *does*

--reasons, that is —

--reasons I'll never be

the kind of man

I would need to be

for her

to need me.

And,

she reasons

that reason

left me

some season

south of the season

she's leaving me

in

and

to;

some season

that feels a fuck of a lot like Winter

looking for reasons

she left,

like seasons

worth living in.

Something you said, I guess, reminded me of

something Pa used to say

Pa used to say

good girls are like cars

you have to warm them up

before you turn them over

And it's the word of the day

over

like over you

and

not really at all

and

still,

which, really, might be tomorrow's word

if tonight stays

still

the way nights since

tend to do

every night

since that last

night

with

you.

Fucker.

Grain.

Let's say I put a grain of sand in a bucket

for every day

since the day

You

left

me.

Mondays and many

means grain and plenty.

One for each day at the window we shared,

looking past the night

until the sun makes it right

another grain and

a Tuesday to follow

another grain and

a little more hollow.

Not the pail, you see

the hollow's in me

The pail's just fine

with the passage of time.

A Wednesday and

a Sunday

and

a grain and a grain

and

again.

Looking out instead of in

for reasons you left me

with buckets of tin.

Words said for Wednesdays

sins are for Sundays

analyzing my dreams

I save for Mondays.

Until the Monday

or the Sunday

you come back to stay —

--all I have left

are things left to say.

That,

and this heavy fucking pail.

Today I spell sadness _ _ _ _ _

(A.I.M.E.E)

And she's sitting across from me,

A.I.M.E.E

and she's

All I May Ever Ever

want

and she's

All I May Ever Ever

need.

And sitting across from her

my eyes say

I want to devour you

and her eyes have

I could run circles around you

written in the circles

the dark of her mascara makes

when she smiles at me,

that

All I May Ever Ever

smile,

bats those

blue

blue

eyes,

breaks my heart clean in two.

So today I spell sadness

A.I.M.E.E

because spelling with those letters

doesn't spell the name of the one

waiting at home

for me to not be

sitting across

from A.I.M.E.E.

And no matter how many ways

I say and spell

words like

I would never do to you

what I'm doing to her,

A.I.M.E.E

and her

blue

blue

eyes

tell me they don't believe me,

don't believe me

because they really, really can't.

And so today I spell sadness

--and she knows the rest—

because I'll never taste

the cotton-candy lip-glossed

cotton candy of her lips

the way I really, really want to.

And the way

the

blue

of her

blue

blue

eyes tells me

she really, really wants me to

too,

knowing that it's wrong and completely

and

impossible and totally.

And today I spell sadness,

right after I spell goodbye

because A.I.M.E.E is leaving

me to memories of tables

and her across from them

one more thing between us

wrong

and

impossible

and

any way you spell it.

Gorillas and Ghosts.

I live on a farm

between gorillas and ghosts.

Ghosts in my head

gorillas in bed

and the ghosts are gorillas

in weight and the way they

weigh on my mind

there in my bed

next to tonight's gorilla

wishing I was beside

a ghost instead.

... Don't Worry Ma; It's A Metaphor

Thoughts of you are razors

across metaphorical wrists.

Yeah, I know it's dark

but you got the light

when you took half,

and all I kept

was your fucking cat.

No further down

How many years

have I wasted

remembering the ten seconds it took

for you to take

my breath and my

heart

and the rest of the half-life

you left me with

when you left me

how many years

ago.

Ten seconds

ten years on

years spent

with the seconds in them

second guessing

the mistake

ten seconds in the making

I made

when I made the choice

ten seconds or ten years

ago;

the choice to let you go;

let you go

knowing I was

nowhere near

man enough

to let you

stay for the seconds

ten, or however many it took

to save years

and my half-life

years on and

no further down the road

you walked away on.

Things I Miss Most

(As Told By the Ten-Year-Old You Turned Me Into)

-your red Skittles smile

-whole football quarters lost beneath covers

-the shampoo I never had the balls to buy on my own

-Everything.

Speaking of Analogies…

I left a light on.

Book 3: For the girl who's stupid enough to stay.

Close that fucking door — there's a draft coming in.

You have to understand,

there's things I miss

and things I don't.

There's places I'll let you take me

places I won't.

Times when I'll feel close to you

others...

sorry, I won't.

So please understand

I'll give you what's left,

closer to half

on account of the hole

the one the One left

when she left out the door.

Please, close it behind you

before asking for more.

You might be taking this the wrong way.

Compliments, to you, are four-letter words

'beautiful' is 'fat'

'lovely' is 'ugly'

and

if you could only see

the look on your face when I

mouth the words

to get you to open yours

around the parts of me you excite most;

And I swear it's exciting

when you swear back

in between words better suited, like

'leave' and you will

and

'fuck you'

like you really, really should.

Of Scars and Ones who Scarred Me.

All I've got

are my scars and the stories

my scars could tell you

of the Ones who scarred me.

There's Ones who smiled

and cut anyway

Ones who warned me they would

and surprised me the same

One who promised they couldn't

as the first knife sunk in

and One who shouldn't

because she was kin.

More buzzwords for broken.

'Clarity' can join 'comfort'

in my little list of words

that mean next to nothing

to my writing

and my relationships.

And

you tell me

my relationship to my writing

is clearly taking

the comfort from us —

--I tell you

--and I'll put it in writing

that 'us' is just ' me'

and

whatever patience I retain today.

And you say I never write about you.

If your name was a color

I'd swear it was my favorite

I might not mention it

but your lips are my favorite, too

I'll never say it

but I think about you

often and only when you're not around;

so the next time you are

around

cross your fingers and find

my arms and my lips

around yours

and

again

and

for real, this time.

Other couples say it's the cutest thing about us!

...

I wear haunted

Like you wear perfume

(so A LOT)

And I'm fine with it

The way you're REALLY, REALLY NOT

Because you're all I've got

And you've yet to realize you could do better.

Truths Rolled In And Around Ego.

You always said

my conscience lived

somewhere south *of my smile;*

and it's that

smile

and things south

that keep you coming

and back;

and on yours

and scratching and clawing

mine,

you swear to me

and

at me

that back is where you'll stay.

Epilogue:

What I've learned, after looking back at all of this…

Fuck.

I really need to get over you.

www.ingramcontent.com/pod-product-compliance
Lightning Source LLC
Chambersburg PA
CBHW020910080526
44589CB00011B/520